How To Celebrate the Winter Solstice

A rational approach
to celebrating the season
without religion

by Thomas Harrop

Whitefish Editions
Lakewood, Colorado
First Edition Published 2012
Copyright © Thomas Harrop, 2012

ISBN: 978-1-300-35177-1
10 9 8 7 6 5 4 3 2 1

Printed in the United States of America
www.celebratethesolstice.com

Table of Contents

Getting Started

C elebrating the seasons and events of the year has been part and parcel of the way people have marked the passage of their lives for millennia. For some of us, the problem is that we believe in science and don't want our celebration to perpetuate traditions that have been harmful to people and society. We also have to decide whether it is harmful to lie to our children. While it seems harmless, the Santa Claus myth is the first time many children learn that their parents have lied to them. Perhaps it is trivial and widespread, but it can have a deleterious effect on a young mind.

This book was created to help people find a comfortable way to approach the mid-winter holiday without the trappings of religion. On the other hand, our intention is not to create another dogma that attempts to control the way you approach the holidays. If you love Santa statues or have a treetop angel that has been in the family for years, don't hesitate to use them. Our hope is that everyone will take our ceremonies, recipes, music and art and make them into a tradition that works for them.

If you choose to just follow these guidelines, that's okay as well. We have attempted to make this a complete holiday package that will satisfy your desire to celebrate in your own way without feeling like you are outside the mainstream of America. Our choices of décor, songs and other tools are all meant to fit in with your friends, family and neighbors and make them comfortable with your celebration even if they follow a different tradition.

We should also stress at this point that we did not set out to reuse parts of established solstice traditions. Like many of you we wanted to find a way to mark the passage of another year and honor our roots on this smallish blue planet. We found that almost all of the ways people have chosen to celebrate involve paganism, Saturnalia or some other religious tradition. We consider all of them to be harmful as they perpetuate beliefs that have no rational basis. It is not necessary to believe is God or forest spirits or anything else that is supernatural to appreciate the fact that our planet operates on a finely tuned and knowable set of principles that support and nurture human and all other life. Occam's Razor teaches us that the simplest solution to a problem is usually correct.

While geology and evolution may seem complicated to the uneducated, they remove the necessity of magic from our lives. In other words, we can choose to believe that life began with one man and one woman (and sons who could only have made other children through incest) or we can believe that life evolved through a process of natural selection where huge amounts of time allowed the human race to develop from other forms of life.

We choose to believe that the great riddles of life can be understood through generations of study and thought and that this is a better way to gain knowledge than studying stories that men from the late stone age used to understand a world that frightened them and filled them with a need to make up powerful allies that, in turn, made them feel less powerless. Isn't it time to leave the cave and enter the age of reason?

Make an Inventory

To get started you should make an inventory of the things you would like to keep from your current tradition. (Don't worry if you don't have any, many people want to make a clean break from their old traditions or simply grew up in a way the didn't provide any guidelines for celebrating the winter holidays.) What holiday songs do you love? What decorations do you have? What holiday foods do you look forward to all year?

If part of your goal is to take religion out of the Solstice celebration, you need to seriously evaluate whether you want to include aspects of your original celebration or make a clean breast of things and move on. I have a collection of "Star Trek" Christmas ornaments. It has taken a while but I am finally putting them in the memory box this year and leaving them out of our celebration. Each year I try to make the whole package more about science and solstice and less about anyone's birth. After all, few theologians actually believe that Christmas is about the birth of their Savior. The fact is that Christians borrowed the holiday to keep people from celebrating a pagan ritual. There never was a war on Christmas, in fact, it was a Christian war on the solstice celebration.

Perhaps you can make a list of all the things you love about the winter holidays and decide to keep a few of them this year. You might find that as you build your new tradition you have less and less need for those things as time passes.

Choose music to set the mood

Which Christmas songs are really just about winter? How about Frosty the Snowman? Deck the Halls? Jingle Bells? All of these are winter songs and some were actually taken from the Solstice tradition originally. It is great to use them and other songs as they were originally intended. Here is one by rock band Jethro Tull. It's on there great "Songs from the Wood" album (This entire album makes a great first collection of solstice music.)

Ring out, Solstice Bells

Now is the solstice of the year,
winter is the glad song that you hear.
Seven maids move in seven time.
Have the lads up ready in a line.

Ring out these bells.
Ring out, ring solstice bells.
Ring solstice bells.

Join together beneath the mistletoe.
by the holy oak whereon it grows.
Seven druids dance in seven time.
Sing the song the bells call, loudly chiming.

Ring out these bells.
Ring out, ring solstice bells.
Ring solstice bells.

Praise be to the distant sister sun,
joyful as the silver planets run.
Seven maids move in seven time.
Sing the song the bells call, loudly chiming.
Ring out those bells.
Ring out, ring solstice bells.
Ring solstice bells.
Ring on, ring out.
Ring on, ring out.

The idea is to find music that will fill your home with harmony, peace and love and that will keep you humming through the longest, coldest nights of winter.

Here are the traditional words to "The Holly and the Ivy":

Holly stands in the hall, fair to behold:
Ivy stands without the door, she is full sore a cold.
Nay, ivy, nay, it shall not be I wis;
Let holly have the mastery, as the manner is.

Holly and his merry men, they dance and they sing,
Ivy and her maidens, they weep and they wring.
Nay, ivy, nay, it shall not be I wis;
Let holly have the mastery, as the manner is.

Ivy hath chapped fingers, she caught them from the cold,
So might they all have, aye, that with ivy hold.
Nay, ivy, nay, it shall not be I wis;
Let holly have the mastery, as the manner is.

Holly hath berries red as any rose,
The forester, the hunter, keep them from the does.
Nay, ivy, nay, it shall not be I wis;
Let holly have the mastery, as the manner is.

Ivy hath berries black as any sloe;
There come the owl and eat him as she go.
Nay, ivy, nay, it shall not be I wis;
Let holly have the mastery, as the manner is.

Holly hath birds a fair full flock,
The nightingale, the popinjay, the gentle laverock.
Nay, ivy, nay, it shall not be I wis;
Let holly have the mastery, as the manner is.

Good ivy, what birds hast thou?
None but the owlet that cries how, how.
Nay, ivy, nay, it shall not be I wis;
Let holly have the mastery, as the manner is.

As you can see, the original lyrics have nothing to do with Christmas. It is, in fact, about a contest between men and women and it predates Christianity by hundreds of years. Holly has been associated with the Solstice since at least Roman times and probably long before that. In fact, the points on the holly leaves were thought to keep away evil spirits so women wore them in their hair during the solstice celebration.

Other than music, feel free to include things like mistletoe (Kissing under this plant was originally a pagan fertility rite.) and burning the yule log (Yule is a Druid word for "wheel" the "Yule Tide" is a reference to the sun, which is shaped like a wheel.) The Christmas tree itself was a tradition in the celebration of mid-winter long before there were Christians.

Most modern Americans have no idea that even in the early colonial period, celebrating Christmas was an offense that would land you in prison. As late as the 1840s the

Christmas tree was reviled as a pagan symbol in America. Not until 1846 when the Queen of England was sketched standing next to an evergreen tree was the Christmas tree even tolerated.

You get the idea by now — as long as you stick to songs about trees and bells and the sun you really can't go wrong.

The Solstice Bell

Although we have been unable to find anything in the ancient traditions that involved the ringing of a bell, we like the idea of marking the exact moment of the solstice this way.

Our family uses a bell inherited from my mother and my mother's mother. In fact, we think the bell has been in the family for more than 100 years. It was never used as a holiday item (It was the bell I rang when I was home from school with some illness or other and I needed my mother's attention.) It brings back great memories to use the bell for this new purpose. If you don't have a "family bell" like mine, get a bell and be the first generation of many to use it for marking the transition from winter to spring.

Many websites provide information regarding the actual time of the winter solstice. www.almanac.com for example gives the time to the nearest minute for the eastern time zone of the United States. Make a note on your calendar and bring the family together (or have them meet over Skype or some other online service) to stage your yearly bell ringing ceremony.

Count down to the moment of the solstice then ring the bell once to mark the moment when the days begin to lengthen into the coming spring. Here are some poems you might read after ringing the bell:

I Heard a Bird Sing

"I heard a bird sing
In the dark of December
A magical thing
And sweet to remember.
'We are nearer to Spring
Than we were in September,'
I heard a bird sing
In the dark of December."
— *Oliver Herford*

The Shortest Day

"So the shortest day came, and the year died,
And everywhere down the centuries of the snow-white world
Came people singing, dancing,
To drive the dark away.

They lighted candles in the winter trees;
They hung their homes with evergreen;
They burned beseeching fires all night long
To keep the year alive,
And when the new year's sunshine blazed awake
They shouted, reveling.
Through all the frosty ages you can hear them
Echoing behind us — Listen!!
All the long echoes sing the same delight,
This shortest day,
As promise wakens in the sleeping land:
They carol, fest, give thanks,
And dearly love their friends,
And hope for peace.
And so do we, here, now,
This year and every year.
Welcome Yule!!"
— *Susan Cooper*

Ring out, Wild Bells

"Ring out, wild bells, to the wild sky,
The flying cloud, the frosty light;
The year is dying in the night;
Ring out, wild bells, and let him die.
Ring out the old, ring in the new,
Ring, happy bells, across the snow:
The year is going, let him go;
Ring out the false, ring in the true."
— *Alfred Lord Tennyson*

Read one of these, or find one that is more suited to the feelings of your family and friends —or write one yourself. The tradition will mean more to you the more you and your family invest in making it. ∎

Preparations for the holiday

About a month before the solstice

Start Decorating

Begin hanging decorations around the house. Things such as candles and incense are nice. Flowers, birds and other hints of the spring to come will make the house feel bright. As the season progresses start adding touches that pay tribute to the sun and her sisters, the stars. Bright colors are the order of the day and help to lighten the mid-winter mood.

Fruits and cookies are good holiday fare. Fruits are especially nice because they are sweet and nutritious and presage the bounty of summer that is just around the corner. We like to have gala apples, oranges and other fruits in a bowl on the table. Berries can also be nice. Again, it is a matter of your family's taste. There is no sense keeping a huge bowl of apples around if they are just going to spoil.

Just before the solstice

Trim the Tree

Evergreen trees have been a staple of the holiday season for millennia. Our family likes to put up the tree and trim it a day or two before the solstice. It helps build excitement and serves as a crescendo for the month long decorating process.

This year we are going to buy a tree from the local nursery and keep it watered and cared for through the holidays. Then we are going to plant it in the yard as a reminder of the holiday season. Keeping your tree this way will add beauty to your yard and prevent the waste of using a tree then throwing it away.

We trim the tree in a sort of modern Victorian style. We collect snowflakes, snowmen, M&Ms and other secular ornaments and add to the collection each year. We also string beads or popcorn and top the tree with a star. Using a realistic sun ornament on top of the tree would be a great way to add a little science to the celebration.

In some traditions, each family member selects a favorite ornament just before the solstice and places it on the tree. You can reserve a selection for this purpose or make ornaments as a family activity and place them on the tree after the bell ringing.

Once the tree is up, we keep it as the centerpiece of our holiday until sometime during the first week of the new year. When we finish with the holiday we take the tree out and plant it in the yard. If you live in a cold climate you should start working on softening the ground at some point or you will have trouble getting the tree planted after the holiday. Last year, we dug a hole in November and put a flower pot upside down in the hole to keep it from caving in. It worked well and we were able to plant the tree in January. It is doing very well.

On the day of the solstice

The Gift Exchange

There is a long raging argument regarding opening Christmas presents on Christmas eve or Christmas day. We don't really care where it came from or why. Again, it should be a family decision. We have to put a word in here about the excitement of waking up to open gifts. It just seems to make the morning and the rest of the day magical. We would love to hear from people who prefer to open on solstice eve.

One other point about gift giving. Much has been made of the fact that Christmas has been corrupted by virtue of having been turned in to an orgy of spending on extravagant presents, on the other hand, Chanukah gifts are often intentionally spartan. Perhaps a good middle ground can be reached. You have to evaluate this for your own family but maybe we can start to bring this under control a little by trying to think of others during the Solstice rather than just thinking of ourselves. Perhaps giving a micro-loan in someone's name or doing something else that is charitable is a good way to show that we value others as much as ourselves. Websites such as www.kiva.org make it easy to make a micro-loan in the name of a friend or loved one.

Nothing makes gift giving more special than gifts that are handmade. If you don't have the time or talent for creating gifts, try www.etsy.com online. This site features the work of crafters and artisans from all over. You can find a unique gift and help support an individual or truly small business. ■

A Time for Reflection

Since the dead of winter is a time that many of us spend indoors it is a great time to engage in reflection about the preceding year and about our lives in general. It is useful and fun to spend time individually or as a family evaluating the course of our lives and making decisions about the direction we should be heading. Most of us will benefit greatly by investing some time and effort in creating a more volition driven life. As Apple founder Steve Jobs said, "Remembering that you are going to die is the best way I know to avoid the trap of thinking you have something to lose. You are already naked. There is no reason not to follow your heart." Are you following your heart? Are you living the life you would choose? Take the opportunity each year to look into your heart and decide.

Once you have made your choices try to put them into action. If your dream is to live in France, try to find a way to make it happen. Most hate and envy come from feelings that we are being cheated out of the life we desire. You can change more things about your life if you have the courage to dream and then follow your dreams.

Write it down

Create a family journal in which everyone can write or draw during the holiday season. This can create a great link between generations in your family. Perhaps you could include friends or pseudo family members as well. I grew up with an uncle named Clare who was in fact just a neighbor that my family included in our life. You don't have to live with a family that doesn't function well because of an accident of birth. Use the solstice as an excuse to become closer to anyone you choose to include in your life.

Buy a special book that can be used year after year without falling apart. As an alternative, get an archival quality box in which you can store loose pages of writing and art. Each year you could search for special papers to add to your collection as part of the celebration.

Holiday Music

Nothing sets the tone for the holidays like music. We have a selection of music by artists like Enya, Jethro Tull and

Mannheim Steamroller. There is a great deal of non-religious music around if you spend some time thinking about it and looking around. In addition to the songs you love there are some great classical pieces and you might even try your hand at writing your own solstice music. It would be a great contribution to the holiday for some great amateur or professional musicians to expand the musical catalog.

See appendix A for music and lyrics to some of our favorites. Our website has our simple recordings of each song (or links to other artists) so that you can get the feeling of the melody.

The iPod is a great accessory for holiday listening. We have a set of speakers into which we plug the iPod and that lets us create a collection of our favorite solstice music. There are a lot of songs that lurk in the middle of a CD somewhere sandwiched between Christmas or other religious music. The iPod makes it easy to filter out the songs you don't want and keep the ones you love.

Keep some song sheets around, too. It may seem corny or '50s to sing holiday songs with the family, but some of my favorite memories growing up came from "Sing-Along with Mitch" or just sing-along with Dad. Even bad singing is fun. If you have a piano or guitar, that's even better. Musical accompaniment can keep everyone on key and on tempo and add some direction to the tune. You might try keeping a collection of instruments around. A wooden recorder, an autoharp and drums are easy to play and make everyone feel included. ■

Readings for the Solstice

I n the Jewish tradition, the Passover Seder is celebrated by the reading of a book called the *Haggadah*. It contains Bible stories about an incident in the history of the Jewish people. We have created some readings that celebrate science and history and help to link you and your family to the intellectual history of the planet. Each year we plan to revise and edit these readings to reflect the cutting edge of thought among the scientists in these fields. We would appreciate hearing from anyone who can add to these readings or make them better present the current state of rational thought about our history.

Welcome to Our Solstice Celebration

Tonight we observe a joyous festival which human beings have likely observed for around 30,000 years. As a people we have been on earth for around 200,000 years and we know that people were looking to the heavens with curiosity and wonder at least 35 millennia ago.

Long ago our species embarked on an important journey. Together with our Neanderthal and Cro-Magnon relatives, we set out to populate and tame a planet which was at the time huge beyond our wildest dreams. From the cradle of civilization in Africa, brave men and women slowly advanced to all points of the compass and to every continent, island and mountain top. Coming from a tiny population we have covered the planet and created myriad societies with distinctive languages and cultures. Tonight we celebrate this huge accomplishment. As we look to the future, we must constantly evaluate, as our predecessors did, what direction is best for our future growth and well being.

Tonight we celebrate life on this planet and the speech and written language that make it possible for us to dream, sing, negotiate, converse, record our thoughts and make notes on our beliefs and understanding of the world.

Ringing in the new season

As we begin our celebration we ring a bell at the moment of the winter solstice. The bell signifies the demarcation between the increasing darkness of winter and the growing light of summer. Each year we recognize this moment to remind ourselves that even in the darkest moments there is always hope for a bright future.

Bringing light to the winter darkness

With candles and decorative lights we dispel the darkness which has been growing and show that our knowledge of the world has grown to the point that we can illuminate the world with understanding.

Light the solstice candles.

May the light of peace and knowledge always keep the darkness that we know the human spirit is capable of at bay. With hope for the future we dream of a world where the energy powering our lights comes from sources that don't hurt the land, the water or the people.

May the light of truth and justice circle the globe and bring us all to the realization that we are all the same under our skin. We hope that next year the world will be a little more educated and little more peaceful. ■

A Solstice Tale

[To be read on the shortest day of the year when all feel that the sun is leaving, never to return. Our tradition is to read this right before dinner.]

 ong ago in a dark cave sat a man, his family huddled behind him near the glowing embers of their winter fire. Thin and dirty he sat wondering for the first time whether the sun might fade away and leave his people in eternal darkness.

For months the sun had been less and less in the sky and on this day, the waning light and heat seemed to come and go before there was time to find food and stoke the fire.

The decision was made to find the largest log the family could carry and bring it back to the cave. The log would burn for days and might provide light and heat were the sun to cease to warm them.

Looking out on the landscape of frost and windswept dirt, it seemed amazing that of all the plants, the evergreen trees never showed the strain of winter cold and wind. The tree seemed to be saying that everything would be fine and the world would continue. After all, how could all life be in jeopardy when this tree remained so constant?

Usually the people took great care with their food because the winter could be long and cold and no one really knew whether food would again spring from the breast of mother earth. Sometimes the plants withered without offering their splendid bounty and other times food was plentiful.

On this night it was decided to feast as if there was no tomorrow because if the sun disappeared, there truly would be no tomorrow. Could the people live in darkness? Would they want to? So it was that they came to eat a feast of their finest sweet and savory foods and they danced and sang in the light of the giant burning log and happiness filled them and replaced the dread they had felt at the loss of their companion star.

As the years rolled on and language began to allow the people to pass on the knowledge of the old ones to the young, a pattern was felt and passed on from one generation to the next. As the year progressed, the sun did indeed show itself for less time until one day it was known was the day on which the sun shown for less time than any other of the year. This day became the day that the people celebrated for they knew that this was just a trick and that the sun was not going to vanish, but simply saved its light and heat to warm the fields of summer when the crops needed it most.

The people marked this 'solstice' (the day when the sun reached its lowest point in the sky) and created a day of remembrance. This day was one of the special days of the year when people came together to rejoice, to remember those who had passed and enjoy those with whom they still shared the journey through life.

For millennia the people have celebrated this night, or a night close to it and brought out their festive clothing, food and drink and shared fellowship and music.

As the people have done for all those years, we do again tonight. So forget your woes and fears, put aside your differences and relish the spirit that fills us all and brings us to this season of joy and wonder at the planet, the animals and plants and the clockwork universe in which we live.

Let us all enjoy the knowledge of our scientists and elders and bring a love of humanity and of learning to the table. Let us share the knowledge we have gained and laugh and joke, tell stories and share the things that make us the same and that make us different.

Just as we share so many traits as human being, we are also individuals, each with a unique story to tell. Let the poet and the bookkeeper and the scientist and the painter and all the others share a love of life and a feeling for the earth that nurtures and provides for us all.

We all live together on this small rock hurtling through space and our fate is intertwined with every other person and animal that shares the land, sea and air.

So, raise a glass to our blue-green home and raise a glass to our fellow travelers, and raise a third to show that you are alive and continuing to learn. For when we cease learning, life is stagnant and without progress.

Tonight we celebrate the shortest day of the year but we know that tomorrow the warmth of the sun's rays will begin a new stage in their yearly cycle and before we know it we will be basking in the full light and heat of the summer sun. Tonight we use the stored energy of our fire to replace the energy of the sun. Tomorrow the sun begins anew and we are grateful for the cycle of the years that reminds us of the cycle of life to which we all belong.

Here is hoping that we will all be here next year to celebrate in love and peace. Those who don't make it will be missed and always remembered. But we always remember that death is a part of life and we remember our departed kith and kin for the way they lived, not their length of their journey with us.

And so on this night, the longest night of the year, we rejoice in the knowledge our greatest thinkers have imparted. We take a break from the routine of our lives and spend it in revelry, thought and laughter.

Eat, drink and be merry — for tomorrow we head back to work and school and the rest of our lives. Tonight we live a few perfect moments together and feel loved and nurtured by each other and the universe. Tonight we are happy and free of the cares of our lives.

And we all say —

We know that the world will be less frightening the less frightened we allow ourselves to be.

Let peace reign in the souls of all who partake of this abundance.

We remember all who are in need and strive to help them be fulfilled.

We will all work to make the world a more loving, kind, cheerful and inclusive place.

We begin to grow the love and caring of the entire planet by giving a heartfelt hug to each person in this room. ■

Time to eat

[This part is to be read after the meal.]

The Beginnings of Conscious Human Life

For more than 30,000 years people have looked at the world around them and asked questions about their life. We know this because it is the sense of wonder in people that makes them create art. Cave paintings, some possibly created using a *camera obscura* technique have been found and dated from about 31,000 years ago and carved figurative art predates that by another 4,000 years.

We are driven to question and our species has developed a system called science to find answers to the great questions that buzz around us like mosquitoes, leaving us no peace until we find solutions for them.

This science we use as a tool to explore and understand our world has a problem. It does not provide final, definitive answers to our riddles. Religion pretends to know all of the answers and presents its solutions to life's great problems as the ultimate authority. The problem with religion is that most of its answers were created during the late stone age or at least the bronze age and they never evolved beyond that time.

Do most people still believe that the world was created in six days, that it is 6,000 years old or that it was once covered in water for more than a month? No, because science has shown us the great beauty of the creation of the earth and its life and there is no need to believe it was a miracle. It took a long time for the earth and it's life to evolve, but it happened through means we can understand. If the earth was flooded for 40 days where did all that water go? We can test and examine and theorize about the possibility of a great flood and we know it could not have happened.

What we do know of the development of the earth and of our species is more wondrous than the creation of life through magic. By understanding the process of evolution, the wonder of geologic time and the history of our race, we can appreciate life in a way that magic does not allow.

In addition, science doesn't try to tell us what life means. No scientist will tell you to dislike one person or another because of the way they live.

And so today we celebrate the knowledge that science has brought us about the proud heritage we share as a human race. We know from genetics that the outward differences we see in Asians, Africans and others are so trivial as to be meaningless. We are all brothers and sisters and we all share a great interest in preserving this planet and maintaining it as a place that makes life feel like it's worth living.

As we celebrate the certain knowledge that the sun will continue in its orbit around the galactic central point, that the earth will continue to orbit the sun and the moon will maintain its path in our gravitational field, we share knowledge that was known to Ötzi, our ancestor from more than 5,000 years ago who most likely understood many of the things we know about the solar year and probably celebrated the solstice, marking the time in his year when the sun would begin to climb higher in the sky, the earth would become warmer and food would be easier to find.

At about the same time Ötzi lived in Europe the Britons began building Stonehenge. This giant ring of stones was likely a calendar that helped the hunter-gatherers of the late stone age make the transition to becoming farmers. The need for tracking the seasons for planting (They couldn't just plant their seeds after Mother's Day like we do) made an astronomical observatory like Stonehenge very valuable. Many theories have come and gone regarding Stonehenge (at one time the Druids were thought to have built it for religious reasons — they didn't) but our best guess now is that people like you and me spent more than 1,500 years building a calendar and timepiece. With all the time and effort they put into this project it must have been important to them.

We have better more portable calendars than Stonehenge now. Atomic clocks can tell us the exact time based on the vibration of atoms. The human race has come a long way. It still has a long way to go.

At this season of renewal and hope for the future, let us commit ourselves to redouble our efforts to make this a world dominated by peace and justice. When you are cut off in traffic, when someone attacks you out of fear or ignorance, try to resist the impulse of your reptilian brain to react in anger.

Promote efforts in civil society to leave the paranoia and greed of the past behind and move the world toward sharing and love.

Show compassion to those who share this planet, whether they are plants, animals or other humans. All life is worth preserving and nurturing. As we learn about this earth, our home, we learn that the mosquito, the wolf, the prairie dog, the mouse and all the other creatures around us are there for a reason. Life exists in a startlingly delicate balance. To hate your enemy, you must really hate yourself. In the end we know that all violence is self destructive.

As we enter a new solar cycle we commit ourselves to renew our spirit and work to make our actions conform to our knowledge of the world. We understand that living in accordance with our beliefs is the only way to relieve the cognitive dissonance in our lives and allow us to be at peace with ourselves and the world around us. ■

Recite this mantra each day as you prepare to face the challenges in your life.

I am a rational being and I know that fear can be overcome by knowledge.

~

I am capable of understanding the world in which I live.

~

I am responsible for my actions.

~

I will offer love to, and accept love from others.

Solstice Carols

Most of us grew up with some sort of religious music for the holidays. It is difficult for me to imagine what it would have been like growing up without a home filled with Doris Day, Perry Como and Mitch Miller during the month of December.

While we eschew religious music these days, music of the winter is wonderful and we love the new carols we have found in the various solstice traditions we have studied. Some of these take a little getting used to, but many of them are very old and connect us to a simpler time in our development as a people.

The Greensleeves Carol

The old year now away has fled
The new year it has entered
Let us now our fears downtread
And joyfully all appear – o
Let's merry be this day
And let us now both dance and play
Kiss, love, cast cares away
To welcome in the New Year

The first day of the year we keep
And we shall never wail or weep
We will good fortune reap
And live with merry cheer – o
Houses now are crowned with thorn
With berry and with ivy – corn
We'll uphold the Wassail horn
To welcome in the New Year

And now with New Year gifts, each friend
His letter doth the other send
We will our comfort lend
And spare not of our gear – o
Like a snake cast off your skin
And to fresh fellow feelings win
Living so you shall begin
To welcome in the New Year

Deck the Halls

Deck the halls with boughs of holly,
Fa la la la la, la la la la.
'Tis the season to be jolly,
Fa la la la la, la la la la.

Don we now our gay apparel,
Fa la la, la la la, la la la.
Troll the ancient Yule tide carol,
Fa la la la la, la la la la.

See the blazing Yule before us,
Fa la la la la, la la la la.
Strike the harp and join the chorus.
Fa la la la la, la la la la.

Follow me in merry measure,
Fa la la la la, la la la la.
While I tell of Yule tide treasure,
Fa la la la la, la la la la.

Fast away the old year passes,
Fa la la la la, la la la la.
Hail the new, ye lads and lasses,
Fa la la la la, la la la la.

Sing we joyous, all together,
Fa la la la la, la la la la.
Heedless of the wind and weather,
Fa la la la la, la la la la.

The Holly and the Ivy

The Holly and the Ivy
When they are both full-grown
Of all the trees that are in the wood
The Holly/Ivy bears the crown

Chorus:
The rising of the sun
And the running of the deer
The rounding of the shining moon
The weary worn hunter

The holly bears a blossom
White as the lily flower
And ivy bears the blackest buds
To pull him to her power

The holly bears a berry
As red as any blood
And ivy bears the greenest leaves
To wrap him in her hood

The holly bears a prickle
As sharp as any thorn
And ivy bears a clinging vine
To smother him right down

The holly bears a bark
Bitter as any gall
And ivy bears small nectar flowers
To sweeten all his fall

The holly and the ivy
When they are both full-grown
Of all the trees that are in the wood
These two shall wreathe as one

Merry Gentlemen
(Tune of 'God Rest Ye Merry Gentlemen')

Now make ye merry, gentlemen
Let winter not dismay
For the sure sun does now return
Upon this very day
To keep us all from dark and cold
He has not gone away

Chorus:
O tidings of comfort and joy,
Comfort and joy,
O tidings of comfort and joy!

Now make ye merry, ladies
Let darkness not affright
For the sure sun does now return
So strong and bold and bright
To keep us all from dark and cold
He has his manly might
Chorus

Now make ye merry, bachelors
Let need not numb your mind
For the sure sun does now return
In fire and flesh and wine
To keep us all from dark and cold
He has a way to find
Chorus

Now make ye merry, maidens
Let damp not spoil your lay
For the sure sun does now return
You'll dance upon the hay
To keep us all from dark and cold
He'll give you what you pray
Chorus

Now make ye merry, children
Let fear not you beguile
For the sure sun does now return
You'll eat and play and smile
To keep us all from dark and cold
There's presents for each child
Chorus

Now to the sun sing praises
All you within this place
And like a loving company
Each other do embrace
The heart felt time of the New Year
Is drawing on apace
Chorus

Frosty The Snowman

Frosty the snowman was a jolly, happy soul,
With a corncob pipe and a button nose,
And two eyes made out of coal.

Frosty the snowman Is a fairy tale, they say,
He was made of snow but the children know
How he came to life one day.

There must have been some magic in
That old silk hat they found.
For when they placed it on his head,
He began to dance around.

Oh, Frosty the snowman was alive as he could be,
And the children say he could laugh and play
Just the same as you and me.

Thumpety-thump-thump, thumpety-thump-thump
Look at Frosty go.
Thumpety-thump-thump, thumpety-thump-thump
Over the hills of snow.

Frosty the snowman knew the sun was hot that day,
So he said, 'Let's run and we'll have some fun
Now before I melt away.'

Down to the village, with a broomstick in his hand,
Running here and there all around the square saying,
'Catch me if you can.'

He led them down the streets of town
Right to the traffic cop.
And he only paused a moment when
He heard him holler 'Stop!'

For Frosty the snowman
Had to hurry on his way,
But he waved goodbye saying,
'Don't you cry,
I'll be back again some day.'

Thumpety-thump-thump, thumpety-thump-thump
Look at Frosty go.
Thumpety-thump-thump, thumpety-thump-thump
Over the hills of snow.

A Wassailing

Here we come a wassailing
Among the leaves so green,
Here we come a wandering
So fair to be seen.

Chorus:
Love and joy come to you,
And to you your wassail too,
And we bless you and send you a happy New Year.
And we send you a happy New Year.

Our wassail cup is made
Of the rosemary tree,
And so is your beer
Of the best barley.
Chorus

We are not daily beggars
That beg from door to door,
But we are neighbors' children
Whom you have seen before.
Chorus

Good Master and good Mistress,
As you sit by the fire,
Pray, think of us poor children
Are wandering in the mire.
Chorus

We have a little purse
Made of ratching leather skin,
We want some of your small change
To line it well within.
Chorus

Call up the Butler of this house,
Put on his golden ring;
Let him bring us a glass of beer,
And the better we shall sing.
Chorus

Bring us out a table,
And spread it with a cloth;
Bring us out a moldy cheese,
And some of your Solstice loaf.
Chorus

We bless the Master of this house,
Likewise the Mistress, too;
And all the little children
That round the table go.
Chorus

Silent Night

by Ellen Reed

Silent night, Solstice Night
All is calm, all is bright
Nature slumbers in forest and glen
'Til in Springtime She wakens again
Sleeping spirits grow strong!
Sleeping spirits grow strong!

Silent night, Solstice night
Silver moon shining bright
Snowfall blankets the slumbering Earth
Yule fires welcome the Sun's rebirth
Hark, the Light is reborn!
Hark, the Light is reborn!

Silent night, Solstice night
Quiet rest 'til the Light
Turning ever the rolling Wheel
Brings the winter to comfort and heal
Rest your spirit in peace!
Rest your spirit in peace!

Let It Snow

Oh the weather outside is frightful,
But the fire is so delightful,
And since we've no place to go,
Let It Snow! Let It Snow! Let It Snow!

It doesn't show signs of stopping,
And I've bought some corn for popping,
The lights are turned way down low,
Let It Snow! Let It Snow! Let It Snow!

When we finally kiss goodnight,
How I'll hate going out in the storm!
But if you'll really hold me tight,
All the way home I'll be warm.

The fire is slowly dying,
And, my dear, we're still good-bye-ing,
But as long as you love me so,
Let It Snow! Let It Snow! Let It Snow!

Jingle Bells

Dashing through the snow
In a one horse open sleigh
O'er the fields we go
Laughing all the way
Bells on bob tails ring
Making spirits bright
What fun it is to laugh and sing
A sleighing song tonight

Oh, jingle bells, jingle bells
Jingle all the way
Oh, what fun it is to ride
In a one horse open sleigh
Jingle bells, jingle bells
Jingle all the way
Oh, what fun it is to ride
In a one horse open sleigh

A day or two ago
I thought I'd take a ride
And soon Miss Fanny Bright
Was seated by my side
The horse was lean and lank
Misfortune seemed his lot
We got into a drifted bank
And then we got upsot

Oh, jingle bells, jingle bells
Jingle all the way
Oh, what fun it is to ride
In a one horse open sleigh
Jingle bells, jingle bells
Jingle all the way
Oh, what fun it is to ride
In a one horse open sleigh, yay!

Welcome Yule

by Norman Iles

Welcome Yule, old heaven's king.
Welcome Yule, born this morning,
Welcome Yule, man full smiling
Welcome, Welcome Yule

Chorus:
Welcome Yule, thou merry man,
Welcome Yule, spend here thy span.
Welcome Yule, thou merry man,
Welcome, Welcome Yule

Welcome Yule, red robéd one,
Welcome Yule, come from the sun,
Welcome Yule, our heart's crimson,
Welcome, Welcome Yule!

Welcome Yule, good news bearer,
Welcome Yule, of the New Year,
Welcome Yule, twelve days you'll hear,
Welcome, Welcome Yule!
Chorus

Welcome Yule, thy log's aflame,
Welcome Yule, thy fire doth gain,
Welcome Yule, warmth grows again,
Welcome, Welcome Yule!

Welcome Yule, enter this hall,
Welcome Yule, centre of all,
Welcome Yule, our first carol,
Welcome, Welcome Yule!
Chorus

Welcome Yule, as ever was,
Welcome Yule, as ever thus,
Welcome Yule, as ever must,
Welcome, Welcome Yule!
Welcome Yule, come well in here,
Welcome Yule, make us good cheer,
Welcome Yule, once more thou'rt here,
Welcome, Welcome Yule!

Carol of the Unconquered Sun

Chorus: Nowell sing we, both all and some,
The sun unconqueréd is come.

He's risen up in love and joy,
Flames out his favour from the sky,
His being brings us gaiety,
Both all and some, both all and some.

Out of the womb of deepest night,
He's sprung with growing warmth and light,
To cure disease and put us right,
Both all and some, both all and some.

The saving sun to us was sent,
To bliss us brought, from blackness bent,
Or else to death we down had went,
Both all and some, both all and some.

Oh, he will shine with love and light,
In furrows fair his pennon strike,
The earth is stirred with lust for life,
Both all and some, both all and some.

Praise to the sun for our comfort,
He's guided us to join his sport,
We'll hold our happiness in his sort,
Both all and some, both all and some.

Recipes

The other great bonding experience of the holidays is food. We always woke up on Christmas morning and had a big family breakfast. Whether you are on your own or having 20 relatives over, food is an important part of the holidays.

Because of concerns for food safety and the chemicals used in foods we currently eat an all plant based diet. We feel that it is healthier and more nutritious. If it is not for you, no problem, just use the traditional ingredients for these dishes. On the other hand, it might not be a bad idea to live for one day or week of the year eating food that is good for you. Also, we have tried all of these dishes and they are very tasty.

Menus

Breakfast

Hot-cross Sun Buns with orange frosting
whatscookingamerica.net/Bread/CinnamonRollsFantastic.htm

Cut up fruit and berries
Mix in some puffed rice cereal, drizzle with real maple syrup and sprinkle on some finely shredded coconut.

Pancakes topped with a fruit solar system (use fruit in the various colors of the planets)

Earth-friendly Pancakes

(makes 6 to 8 pancakes)

2 cups all-purpose unbleached flour

1 tsp. baking soda

1 tsp. baking powder

1 tsp. kosher salt

1 Tbs. organic sugar

2 cups almond, soy, oat or other non-dairy milk

2 Tbs. unsweetened organic applesauce

Directions: Preheat griddle to 350°F. Whisk together dry ingredients (flour through sugar). In a separate bowl, whisk together milk and applesauce. Pour the wet ingredient into the dry ingredients. Stir until just combined. Do not over mix. Let batter rest for about 5 minutes.

Lightly grease griddle with neutral high-heat vegetable oil, or a buttery spread like Earth Balance. Ladle batter onto griddle — about three tablespoons per pancake. Turn pancakes when the edges start to look dry and bubbles appear on top.

Celebration Meal

Meat-like substance
Field Roast Celebration Roast, available in 1- and 2-pound versions (www.fieldroast.com)

Sweet potatoes
Mashed sweet potatoes baked with orange juice, maple syrup, Earth Balance and a dash of cinnamon (optional)

Cranberry Sauce
Homemade cranberry sauce is delicious and nutritious — very different than that can-shaped gel we grew up with.

Orange Cranberry Sauce

10 ounces fresh or frozen cranberries

1/4 cup sweet red wine or cranberry juice

1/4 cup fresh orange juice and some zest from the peel

1/2 cup real maple syrup (grade B is best!)

1/2 cup raw honey or agave nectar

optional: 1/2 tsp. cinnamon, 1/4 tsp. cloves, 1/4 tsp. ginger; 1 apple, like Gala or Red Delicious, chopped.

Directions: Combine all ingredients in a medium sauce pan. Bring to a gentle boil over medium low heat, stirring frequently. When cranberries begin to soften, start crushing them with the back of a spoon. Continue cooking and crushing until the sauce starts to thicken (about 10-15 minutes). The sauce thickens even more as it cools. Store in a glass jar in the refrigerator, or freeze for long-term storage

Drinks

Wassail

6-inch stick cinnamon

12 whole cloves

6 cups water

12 ounces cranberry juice

12 ounces raspberry juice

12 ounces apple juice

1 cup peach juice

1/3 cup lemon juice

1/4 cup agave nectar

Directions: Make a spice bag by cutting a 6-inch square of double thickness cheesecloth. Place cinnamon and cloves in center of square, bring up corners, and tie closed with a clean kitchen string. In a 4- to 6-quart slow cooker, combine water, juices and agave. Add the spices. Cover; cook on low heat setting for 4 to 6 hours or on high heat for 2 to 3 hours. Remove spice bag and discard. Ladle into glasses

Hot Chocolate

2-1/2 cups almond milk

3 Tbsp. raw agave nectar

3 Tbsp. organic cocoa powder

1/2 tsp. sea salt

1/2 tsp. vanilla extract

1 pinch ground cinnamon

Directions: Bring the almond milk, agave, cocoa powder, salt, vanilla extract and cinnamon to a simmer in a saucepan over medium-high heat. Remove from the heat and whisk until frothy. Serve immediately.

Dessert

Pumpkin Pie

1 unbaked 9-inch pie shell (we make the pie crust with Earth Balance Organic Coconut Spread instead of shortening)

2 hand raised chicken eggs

1 15-ounce can organic pumpkin

3/4 cup sugar

1/2 tsp. sea salt

1 tsp. ground cinnamon

1/2 tsp. ground ginger

1/4 tsp. cloves

12 ounces full-fat coconut milk

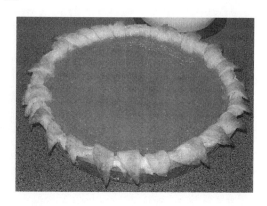

Directions: Preheat oven to 425°F. In a small bowl, lightly whisk eggs. Place all ingredients into the bowl of a stand mixer and blend until homogeneous, scraping the bowl sides down a couple of times to get all the spices off the sides. You can stir it all by hand it you don't have a mixer.

Pour the mixture into the pie shell. Leave at least 1/4 inch of empty space in the pie shell because the mixture will rise a little bit. Bake 15 minutes at 425°F, then reduce temperature to 350°F and bake for 45 more minutes. We like to let the pie chill overnight in the refrigerator because the flavors seem to blend better.

Top with whipped HealthyTop (made by MimicCream) www.mimiccream.com. (This topping actually is tastier than dairy whipped cream. It also whips faster and easier, stores longer without spoiling, and is better for your body than dairy. It's a real win win win!)

Banana Cinnamon Streusel Muffins
Makes about 18 dairy-free, egg-free, nut-free muffins
Streusel:
3/4 cup unbleached flour
1/2 cup organic brown sugar
1 Tbs. cinnamon
6 Tbs. margarine *
Cake:
1 box of Cherrybrook Kitchen yellow cake mix (cherrybrookkitchen.com)

3/4 cup water

3 ripe medium-size bananas, mashed

3 Tbs. margarine, melted

1 tsp. cinnamon

Directions: Preheat oven to 350°F. Lightly oil muffin tins (organic coconut oil works great if you like the flavor)

Combine first four streusel ingredients in a bowl (flour through cinnamon) and then cut in margarine to make crumbs. Set aside.

In a large mixing bowl, combine mashed bananas, melted margarine, cinnamon and cake mix. Batter will be fairly thick. Ladle about 1/4 cup into each muffin cup and top with streusel mixture. Bake about 25-30 minutes or until a toothpick inserted into the center of a comes out clean.

* You may substitute butter, if desired.

Snacks

Baked pie crust strips with sugar and cinnamon

Take leftover pie crust dough after making a pumpkin pie and cut it into strips. Sprinkle a mixture of sugar and cinnamon over the dough and bake for 15 minutes at 350°. Allow the strips to cool and eat like cookies. (This was a treat my mother always used to make for us.)

Toasted nuts

Walnuts, Almonds, Pecans, Cashews, Filberts, Macadamias, etc. Drizzle nuts with melted Earth Balance buttery spread or neutral oil, sprinkle with either salt & pepper or sugar & cinnamon and toast in the oven.

Fruit
Cut any variety of ripe fruit into various shapes.

Veggie chips
We like Beanfields' bean & rice chips — or make your own. Here is a recipe for making homemade chips: www.chow.com/recipes/29591-sweet-potato-crisps

Homemade apple crisps

Apple Chip Recipe
from Ontario Apple Growers (www.onapples.com)

2 large apples

2 Tbsp. sugar

1 tsp. cinnamon

Preheat oven to 200°F. Thinly slice apples crosswise about 1/8-inch (2 mm) thick with a mandolin or sharp knife. Arrange apple slices in a single layer on two parchment lined rimmed baking sheets. In small bowl, combine sugar and cinnamon. Put mixture into a sieve and sprinkle evenly over apple slices. Bake in the top and bottom third of the oven until apples are dry and crisp, about 2 hours. Remove from oven and let 'chips' cool completely before transferring to a sealed container for up to three days. Makes about 2 cups.

Activities

These days it seems like people are never really together. Sitting in a meeting the other day, I suddenly realized I was with 10 colleagues and every one of them was either using their laptop or texting. We need to have a day when we put all that away and just spend time together.

This section is filled with activities the family can do together without using computers. It may seem archaic to your children, it may seem like torture, but we hope it will allow you to spend some time together actually talking and making things rather than just sharing space and radio waves.

Candle Making

The craft of candle making dates back at least 5,000 years and probably much longer. In ancient times, candles were made out of a variety of materials from rolled up papyrus and rice paper to boiled cinnamon tree fruit and even wax from insects combined with seeds. We don't know where candles came from, but they have almost always played a part in our celebrations.

In the middle ages most candles used around the house were made from animal fat (tallow) which gave off an acrid smell and created smoke which got onto everything in the house. Churches and the wealthy used beeswax candles because they smell nice and don't smoke.

Candle making continues to be a popular undertaking even in the age of the light bulb. In the 1990s, a resurgence in the popularity of candles for the home lead to advances such as soybean wax and palm oil wax which both remove the need for petroleum in the making of candles, creating a clean and renewable source of wax for the future.

The secret to modern candle making is learning to combine the various types of wax, wicks and scents to create a candle that burns brightly and last as long as possible. There are many craft shops on the internet, and probably in your local area that can provide the materials and knowledge you need to make beautiful candles for your home and for your holiday celebrations. Just remember that when you use candles they are on fire, they should be used with care and not left burning unattended.

Make Solstice Cards

Giving and receiving cards is a great to let the people in your life know that you are thinking about them. We have a memory box filled with cards from years of holidays and some of the most special are the hand colored beauties made by our children when they were very young.

Hand crafted cards range from simple Crayolas on paper to elaborate cards cut with stencil machines and layered like museum pieces. Whatever you choose to create, the recipient will be pleased to know that you cared enough about them to spend time making something for them instead of buying something mass produced.

One of our favorite hand made cards is created by trimming a photo to fit on a hand decorated card, then gluing it in place with glue stick, spray adhesive or double-stick tape. Remember, you are probably not making something that will have to last for decades. If the card makes it through the season that is usually enough.

Our friend uses a stencil cutter to make cards and has a great time designing and creating very elaborate cards with personalized messages. These machines made by companies such as Cricut and Fiskars help you create professional-looking results by hand. They are simple to use and make a great family project. In addition to holiday cards you can use them for school projects, business thank-you notes and scrapbooking.

Write about or draw pictures of the things you love about family, friends, and the earth.

What makes your life fun and worthwhile?

The holiday seasons are great times to reflect on the meaning of your life. It can be a time to look back at the past year to decide what is working in your life and what isn't working. It is also a great time to look forward to the coming years and put yourself on a course that works for you and your family.

A family journal can be a great way to express these feelings and ideas and keep them safe and available. Perhaps you should review this journal every month or so to remind you of the things you thought were worthwhile and to provide an emotional anchor when things are not going the way you want them to go.

It might be easier for younger family members to draw or for someone to help them get their feelings down on paper in the journal. Why not create a place in the house where your book and a writing implement are always available? Family members can record their thoughts and feeling on an ongoing basis. It would be like a family diary.

You can also record facts and dates like people used to do in their family Bible. What a treasure this will be when the family is grown if you have one place where you kept track of every new tooth, heights and favorite foods, the first girlfriend and all those things that we always wish we could remember.

The important thing is to stay with it. Once you start doing a journal it will only be valuable if you use it. Perhaps you can make a time each week or month for family to put down their thoughts. Keeping the journal online might see cool and modern, but what happens when the site where your journal is kept goes out of business? We think it's better to keep valuable family memories in the analog world where the family actually lives.

Analog Games

We have nothing against video games (Well, that might not be quite true.) but they tend to keep people apart, rather than together. While games such as Wii bowling can be great family activities, first person shooters tend to isolate rather than bring us together.

Why not pull out the old games. Games like Risk and Stratego teach valuable problem-solving skills; Scrabble is a fine vocabulary builder; many card games are great for the family, and we could go on and on. Some of our favorites are Othello, Monopoly and the game of Life. What games did you grow up playing?

Another thing that makes these games special for us is finding old original versions of the games on Ebay. We have purchased Scrabble and Risk with the original wooden pieces (They are much nicer to hold and use than the cheap plastic pieces.) and Monopoly games that were made within the first few years the game was on the market.

These 'antiques' link us to our past, and the common past of many Americans. You might be surprised how many smiles you elicit when you bring out a complete copy of the 'Cootie' game.

Whatever you decide to play, keep it friendly and family. It's more important to teach love and support and provide a safe environment than to be the winner at Monopoly. Try to communicate to your family that you are creating memories, which are the most important thing you can have as you pass through this world.

Maybe you can find a new game each year and learn it together. Card games like Rook and Racko are great for families and old games such as Backgammon and Chinese Checkers let the whole family play together. If you don't have the money to head to the store (or Ebay) every time you need a game try learning card games. Our friends love Hearts and Spades and a deck of cards is only a couple of dollars. You might also find some lovingly used games at the thrift store or a garage sale.

We hope your family enjoys years of great solstice celebrations. It might seem a little odd to be celebrating a different holiday during the end of December, but we believe that it will be worth a little adjustment to get humanity off its 'magic' jones.

It's probably best to view your first couple of years as a settling in period. It takes a while for family and friends to get used to the change. With our family, though, it took less time than we expected.

We would really like to hear your experiences, your successful and not so successful events and ideas as well as the things that you love and would like to share with us. If you have a correction to our science, please let us know. Got a great recipe you think people will want to add to their celebration? Ditto. We want to turn the secular celebration of the holidays into a movement and we need your feedback to do that.

Please share these ideas with your friends and family. We would appreciate it if they buy their own copy of this book as it helps us keep some cash flow so we can work on other holidays and celebrations.

Watch for another book that deals with the summer solstice and a third that provides a secular approach to events such as weddings, births and baby naming.

With the help of a strong community we can bring reason, which is badly needed, to the world in which we all find ourselves.

Enjoy the solstice! ∎

Made in the USA
Middletown, DE
10 December 2014